Born Into Crime

Second Edition

Louise Hansen

Born Into Crime

Louise Hansen

Copyright © 2023

All Rights Reserved

Born into Crime

Dedication

This compelling story is influenced by a true story that entertains the imagination.

An intriguing page-turner, dedicated to all who fought for the life they desire.

Born Into Crime

Lacey's Family & Acquaintances

Merlin .... Dad

Pamela .... Stepmom

Beatrice .... Mom

Minnie .... Grandma
*Beatrice's Mom

William .... Uncle
*Beatrice's Brother

Franklin .... Stepdad
*Beatrice's 2nd Husband

Layla .... Aunt
*William's 1st Wife

Diana .... Aunt
*William's 2nd Wife

Sarah Lane .... Friend from College

Inspector Lane .... Sarah's Father

Eliza Tobias .... Elder Ancestor

Approximately two hundred years ago, Eliza began the trend of only Women being able to call upon the powers of Morgana in the Tobias family.

Arthur .... Elder Ancestor

*And the first Tobias Family member to receive power from Morgana. Morgana is not from this corporeal realm and is the source and benefactor of the Tobias family's power for many generations to come.

Morgana .... Dark Entity

Marked Arthur with the Pentagon of Morgana, revealing the secrets of witchcraft and providing him with dark powers that the normal mind of a mortal couldn't even fathom.

Mr. Smith .... Minie's next-door Neighbor

Gale .... Lacey's new apartment Neighbor

Born into Crime

Acknowledgment

This story was influenced by a true story with exciting added details that will entertain the imagination.

Born into Crime

About the Author

Louise Hansen lives in the Metropolitan Detroit area where she was born and raised. She began writing in 1976, believing she could make a difference by impacting the literacy world. All the while enjoying her journey with family, friends and helping others.

Born into Crime

Contents

Born into Crime

This compelling story will entertain the imagination with unexpected events and excitement.

An intriguing page-turner, dedicated to everyone who fought for their freedom.

Chapter 1

Born into Crime

Lacey's Life

The world is a dark and mysterious place. It is filled to the brim with unsolvable curiosities and deadly secrets. It is a malevolent mechanism. These were all thoughts swirling around the very annals of Lacey's mind as she struggled to grasp the reality that was facing her.

Lacey was born into a life of crime. Her fate was seemingly unknown in the face of this reality. But what were the events in her life that made her face this truth? Let's step back into her past and see what cards Lacey was dealt with and what path she chose when faced with the ultimatum of embracing her sinister roots or forging an entirely new path for herself in her father's spirit.

Lacey's Life

The roots of Lacey's ties to crime can be traced from her mother's side; witchery had been practiced for centuries with information from books written with incantations and spells dated back from the middle 1800s that were passed down from generation to generation all the way to her when she was in her late 20's. Throughout these dark decades, her ancestors committed many crimes that had gone cold, as is the nature of witchcraft; no mortal truly understands what it entails or means. This is why the nature of her family was always under wraps from the rest of the world, which was oblivious to the crimes that took place, with what seemed like no rhyme or reason.

Tracking back this part of her history, it all began for her with her grandmother, Minnie. She seemed inconspicuous enough, as long as you were only watching from a distance. Her looks deceived her true nature, for how on Earth would one assume that this timid, seemingly sweet woman would even think of evil acts? One could believe she would drop by just to give you cookies! But as was said before, looks can be deceiving. She had long been entrenched in the world of witchcraft. Her talons fully sank into the dark arts to commit multiple atrocities in the name of her

Lacey's Life

personal interests.

Lacey's mother's extended family using their incomprehensible power came in an event from her childhood. She remembers what her uncle, William, did. She won't ever forget what he did with his powers.

William, like his mother Minnie, seemed to have inherited the seemingly friendly visage she wore. But just like his mother, numerous dark powers were playing their hand behind their demeanor. William was married to a woman named Layla. They were married for a short while up until her '*Untimely passing.*' That's what the world was told, but Lacey knew; Lacey remembered. William had found Layla to be cheating on him one day, and in a fit of rage, William snuffed out the flame of her life just like that. William was 6'4" with a large build and a broad, muscular body. He served four years in the Army. After being discharged from the United States Army, he began installing different types of flooring for residential and commercial properties. The rage he had about Layla, the woman he was married to, being with another man was like an ice pick that ran through his brain and changed his perception to extremely dark with the flick of a switch.

Lacey's Life

He viciously beat the life out of her, not even thinking about any dark incantations to make it discreet. No, he took a baseball bat to her head multiple times so he could relish in her suffering. Although, that wasn't where the trail of insanity ended; even after he killed her, not for a second did he feel any remorse. Instead, he began making plans to ensure he would receive the most he could out of the cold murder of his wife.

William wanted to sell his house, which he owned with Layla. He also wanted to get rid of her body. That was the beginning of his new plans to destroy and rebuild the built-in pool in the backyard. Plans to make a larger built-in pool began 48 hours later. Of course, to enlarge the pool, all the concrete needed to be broken and removed.

The night before the new concrete for his larger pool was to be poured, he buried her body in the new pool hole. While enjoying his coffee the next morning, he stood by his kitchen window, smiling as the concrete was poured into the newly designed built-in pool.

He was happy to get back to work without that woman and without any embarrassment. When his family or friends asked about Layla, he would explain that she had left him, and he had no idea where she was. He

Lacey's Life

saved Layla's ID and other identification because he wanted to sell the house. This way, he could leave the property and move on with a lady who would be faithful and start a family.

It wasn't long before he began dating again. He met Diana while installing new flooring in her mother's home. A few months later, he wanted to ask Diana to marry him. He asked his sister Beatrice, Lacey's mother, who earned a living as a hairdresser, to help him. William asked his sister to do Diana's hair and makeup to look like Layla.

This was important because he wanted Diana to impersonate Layla at the closing of the sale of the house owned by the two. Soon afterward, William and Diana had a fake wedding in a church with family and friends (without a Marriage License, of course). As was in their nature, Lacey's grandmother and mom also knew and lied to the rest of the world so society would believe they were legally married. They still cared about their image of being the perfect family. They snuffed out a human life and treated the entire situation like it was just another Tuesday. Beatrice had a very neutral look about her. Merlin was her first love and was Lacey's biological father. A couple of

Lacey's Life

years after Lacey's conception, their relationship soured. Merlin was one with his higher power, as is common practice in the American Indian indigenous people. They have strong ties to the righteous path that had been paved for them by their ancestors. This fact was just one of the multiple points of contention Beatrice and Merlin had. Another was that Minnie, acting as the devil on Beatrice's shoulder, constantly voiced her distaste and disapproval of Merlin. She left no stone unturned to try and ruin Merlin with her witchery, but it seemed Merlin's connection to his higher power stood strong, shielding him from her attempts.

All of this came to a head when Lacey was two years old. Merlin and Beatrice decided they had had enough and got a divorce, considering it in everyone's best interests. They forgot their daughter, discarding her thoughts and feelings to the wind. Lacey was confused, but what could she have done? She was only two years old. Life went on from that point, with Merlin having his visits and Minnie's face souring at just the sight of him. But when Lacey turned four, a harrowing incident occurred, which sits with her to this day. Minnie decided that Merlin was a threat to

Lacey's Life

the family's very existence. He was the antithesis of their way of life. This was a reason for Minnie's hatred toward Merlin and his presence with Lacey. Minnie and Beatrice thought they had finally gotten rid of Merlin after the divorce, but Lacey was acting as an anchor for him.

So, she thought, "*What if I get rid of the anchor?*" She then set into motion her sinister plan. Minnie told Beatrice that the only way to get rid of Merlin was to get rid of Lacey for good.

The plan was simple. Lacey was made to stand by the side door of Minnie's house. In front of the side door were the basement stairs. Minnie waited until Lacey was not paying attention to her surroundings. With a sudden jerk, she violently pushed Lacey down the stairs. According to Minnie and Beatrice, this act of malice was a necessity. Her body viciously tumbled and collided with the steel edges of the stairs. She repeatedly yelled, "*Owe!*" when her body hit the cement floor at the bottom of the stairs, she lost consciousness.

To the dismay of Minnie and Beatrice, Lacey survived. Perhaps seeing the sad state of her little body spurned the little bit of humanity they still had in themselves

Lacey's Life

as they decided it might be best to take her to the doctor. It was a simple enough cover-up story as she was getting stitched up. *"Oh, she just fell down the stairs, that's all. You know how kids are,"* Beatrice explained, trying to seem relatable but coming off as very robotic to the doctor, who could sense there was something off about the whole situation. He still did not have evidence of the contrary and decided to treat the child as an accident victim.

The doctor questioned in his own mind, *"How could a child fall down a flight of stairs THIS violently?"*

The procedure was done fairly quickly, as was their swift return to their house, where Beatrice cut Lacey's hair short so no one would notice when the hair grew back by where the doctor needed to shave it to stitch her skin on her head. After many delegations, it was decided that there was only one way to go back to how things were. They decided to resort to the dark arts once more. They cast a dark spell on Lacey, forcing her to forget this event. It was agreed that they would never speak about this again.

Beatrice began dating again when Lacey was eight years old with a man named Franklin. They decided to mimic how her brother William was married because

Lacey's Life

Franklin killed his wife for her life insurance money and sole ownership of the house they owned. The hospital had recorded the cause of death as unknown because they could not understand why each of her organs began to fail one after another. Back in the 1970s, a lot of poisons were not detected in the medical field, even during an autopsy. Nevertheless, Beatrice and Franklin had a fake wedding in the same church where her aunt and uncle had their fake marriage. Not needing a marriage license was a way to avoid the radar of legalities. This, just like all the other tragic events in Lacey's short life span, affected her greatly, but it was a bit of a blessing from one angle, too.

A year after the start of her mother's new relationship, Lacey turned nine years old and was allowed to see Merlin, her father, more frequently. Lacey's dad brought her close to her higher power. Together, they prayed and enjoyed blessings. They both enjoyed listening to music, and they both played different instruments. Merlin played the drums, and Lacey played the flute. It was perhaps one of the only times Lacey felt genuinely happy. She never wanted to leave when the time came around, but alas, she was

Lacey's Life

always forced to go back to her mother's family.

Lacey never felt like she belonged with her mother and her mother's side of the family. She always felt like an outsider, like a foreign entity in the very family she was born into. When she started spending more time with her father and her father's side of the family, she understood where she came from and enjoyed feeling connected with a family who loved her the way she wanted to be loved. These moments kept Lacey from spiraling into the same path her mother's family had walked on. Life went on as Lacey grew into her own. She took her father's teachings to heart and, on the inside, shunned her mother's side of the family. Uncle William, Grandma Minnie, her stepfather Franklin, and even her mother, Beatrice, had all become strangers in her heart. One day, when she was twelve years old, while visiting with her father, she began to remember what had happened to her when she was small. She remembered hearing her mother and grandmother discussing how to eliminate her father's presence by ending her life. Her father saw the shocked look on her face and asked her what was wrong. She decided not to tell her father, knowing it would tear him apart inside.

Lacey's Life

On the way back home, she started recalling more harrowing incidents. Her mind flashed to the incident where Minnie and Beatrice were arguing, and for the first time in all these years, she could recall them discussing ways to get Merlin to stop coming over. She heard their plan that day but had repressed it, for the thought of it was too painful. She was unaware that her grandmother and Mother cast a dark spell on her to forget this happened.

The moment she got back home to her mother's house, she went to her mother and began telling her that she remembered the discussion between her and her grandmother about eliminating her father from their lives by attempting to murder her by violently pushing her down the basement stairs at her grandmother's home. Lacey screamed at her mother, *"How could you do that to me and tell me you love me my entire life?"*

Beatrice immediately became angry and said, *"I don't know what you're talking about."* She refused to continue the conversation and yelled back at Lacey to get out of her face.

Beatrice's dismissal of Lacey shattered her reality. Lacey thought to herself, "Does my mother really

Lacey's Life

care that little about me?" Her mother seemed to be using the same tactic she and Minnie used on everyone else: dissociating from the situation and continuing the façade of presenting themselves to the public as being considerate, friendly, and trustworthy. A testament to this tried-and-true tactic lay in the fact that Neighbors and friends would describe her mother, stepfather, grandmother, aunt, and uncle as some of the nicest people they had ever met.

The years went on, and Lacey was dismissed every time she tried to talk with anyone about any of the criminal activities she learned had happened from her elders over the years because everyone believed all of Lacey's elders were the nicest people. At this point, Lacey decided it was best to watch her own back and enjoy her life while growing up by pretending all was nice and happy in her life.

Making friends at school and in her neighborhood. However, Lacey remembered what her family had made her go through. She kept that in the back of her mind.

Lacey remembered everything.

Chapter 2

Born into Crime

Staying Quiet

The strength of the Tobias Family lay in the fact that they were hidden in plain sight. Although all the signs were already there for the world to see, it was almost as if everyone was blinded by a spell, one that caused them to be unable to see the obvious crimes committed by the Tobias Family.

Although, it holds true when they say that no good deed goes unpunished. This was a fact that Lacey Tobias had made synonymous with her way of life. Her mother's family spared no leniency when it came to disciplinary correction for the children of the family.

Just to clarify, these weren't the run-of-the-mill punishments normal folk would have for their children, like timeouts and grounding. A sinister family would, of course, have a sinister form of punishment. These punishments took various forms,

Staying Quiet

ranging from but not limited to beatings with a wooden spoon or belt, eating soap, and sometimes, not eating at all. These punishments were harsher if any children questioned any of the "advice" handed out by their elders. Mind you, advice is being used very loosely because the word of the elders was the word of truth.

This all led to Lacey being more than capable of holding her tongue in silence. Throughout the first decade of her life, she knew she was not safe at all because of these punishments. This was especially true if she didn't follow rules or talk when not spoken to. The elders clearly stated to all the Tobias children that adult conversations were none of their business. If the adults stopped talking about it, the children would not speak even a whisper of it.

Every child in this family knew if they ever repeated anything they heard or saw, good or bad, and without permission from an elder who was involved, the punishment would be more than a beating. Despite the wonderment of a child when they saw something that could not be explained, they had to hold their tongue lest they risk a thorough 'disciplinary correction.'

Staying Quiet

This all culminated in a vicious cycle within the Tobias Family, where violence bred violence, as the children had grown accustomed to the hurling of insults toward them.

Lacey seemed to be an exception to this violence, as she had a strong, willful disposition toward the atrocities committed by her mother's side of the family. Her distaste for them and their ways must have stemmed from the attempt on her life her grandmother and mother made all those years ago. But ultimately, they were still a family to her. In her mind, it was best to let it go and forgive them.

One fateful day, Minnie was leaving for an unspecified trip over the coming winter months and asked Lacey to take care of her apartment. She was moving out due to the death of her second husband. This may sound like an inconspicuous enough task for any normal family, but the Tobias family always had a way to make life more complicated.

One morning, Lacey decided to clean the place when she noticed the tables and shelves were gathering dust. She was cleaning away all day, making sure Minnie didn't have a reason to give her an earful when she was back. This led to a harrowing discovery for

Staying Quiet

Lacey as she traversed the dark web of her family's history yet again. There was a sheet of paper on the last desk she was dusting. It wasn't just any ordinary paper, though. It appeared to be a list of everyone in her family with their date of birth, social security number, and life insurance information.

Lacey couldn't help but think, "What the hell even is that?" Reading through the list brought her closer and closer to one conclusion: Minnie had cashed a life insurance policy for every relative who had died. Lacey kept thinking, "Where do these people even draw the line?" The differentiating line between sorcery and crime continuously grew blurrier and blurrier as she started connecting the dots.

"How many of my relatives actually knew about all this, and if they did, who were they?" Lacey couldn't help but think.

She felt almost as if she was going to faint. The weight of her ancestors' transgressions hit her like a bullet train. She felt the urge to scream out to the world about how her family wasn't what the world thought it was. However, she knew that these cries for help would simply sink into an endless void of lies and deceit.

Staying Quiet

She took a few deep breaths and thought to herself, "Calm down, Lacey, deep breaths. You've been through worse." For indeed, she had been through worse, but the compounding of all her emotions led to a burden she could no longer take, as she decided to call her confidant Sarah Lane, a college friend who had become Lacey's closest friend and outlet for all her grievances.

They were extremely close, so much so that Sarah was the only other human on Earth outside the Tobias Family besides Merlin to know of their dark nature.

"Hey, you're not busy right now, are you?" Lacey asked.

"Oh god, you're being formal. What did Minnie do this time?" Sarah responded, seemingly already familiar with Lacey's song and dance by now.

"It's not just grandma anymore, Sarah. I'm afraid I've found something much worse. It's a whole list of people from the Tobias lineage. From what I can tell, most of them are deceased, with the red ink used to cross their name out. I think Minnie and the rest of the family are banking on their deaths to claim the life insurance," Lacey explained.

Staying Quiet

Sarah was at her wit's end. Every encounter with the Tobias Family seemed to take a darker turn, leaving her with a burning frustration she could no longer contain. She implored Lacey, "Why does it seem like things only get worse when we deal with them? Lacey, please seriously consider what I've said. We should really go to the police. They need to face the consequences for their actions." A fire raged inside Sarah, fueled by the painful memories of her own family's victimization at the hands of the Tobias Family.

Her father had been an investigator, once relentlessly pursuing leads that could bring down the Tobias Family. Minnie, a sinister Tobias clan member, sensed his growing proximity to the truth and resorted to dark magic to thwart his efforts. The morning after, he was discovered lifeless in their basement, bearing ominous signs of strangulation. The case took a grim turn when authorities seemingly concluded that Detective Lane had taken his own life by hanging himself.

At the time, Sarah was too young to comprehend the depths of the conspiracy. However, as Lacey confided in her about their shared past, the puzzle pieces began

Staying Quiet

to fall into place. "Sarah, you know I can't just go to the authorities. If anything happens to them, I'd be an accessory to their crimes and face punishment too," Lacey attempted to pacify Sarah, although deep down, she knew this was far from the truth. Lacey clung to the hope of redeeming her mother's side of the family, an earnest desire to rescue her own kin.

Losing her patience, Sarah exclaimed, "Lacey, it's your call, but you can't keep justifying and defending those monsters. They're beyond redemption!"

With a sigh, Lacey responded, "I understand, I really do. Let's give it some time to gather more concrete evidence, alright?"

Reluctantly, Sarah agreed. "Alright, Lacey, I've got to run now. I'm running late for some errands. Take care, and remember, I always have your back," she assured her.

"Thank you, Sarah. See you later. Bye," Lacey hung up, her voice tinged with a hint of relief. Yet, as she took a picture of the damning list and held it close, she couldn't shake the growing realization that the Tobias Family's time of reckoning was imminent. She was determined to ensure she had something on them

Staying Quiet

when that day arrived, and the secrets they held would be exposed.

Chapter 3

Born into Crime

Unsolved Crimes

Wherever the Tobias family went, they left a trail of mystery behind them. It was bad due to the number of crimes they committed over their long history. All of the murders and dark happenings that surrounded their very existence seemed to elude the authorities.

That does beg the question, though, how *were* they left undetected?

Well, the Tobias family had their ways.

Hidden from the prying eyes of the world, the Tobias family honed their craft for generations. It all began with the storied tale of Arthur Tobias, a lowly peasant in Crestwood's small, medieval village, nestled in the heart of the 15th century.

Arthur was known for his unassuming appearance, with a mop of unruly brown hair and a perpetually dirty set of clothes. He lived a modest life, toiling in the fields from dawn till dusk to support his elderly,

Unsolved Crimes

just-as-unassuming parents.

One fateful day, as Arthur wandered deeper into the forest, searching for edible herbs to supplement his family's meager meals, he stumbled upon a hidden glade. Within this glade, he encountered a mysterious old woman with piercing blue eyes and a gnarled staff, who introduced herself as Morgana. Unbeknownst to Arthur, Morgana was a dark entity, not from this corporeal realm, the source, and benefactor of the Tobias family's power for many generations to come.

Morgana saw something in Arthur, a hidden potential that could be harnessed. It decided to mark him with *the Pentagon of Morgana*, revealing the secrets of witchcraft and providing him with dark powers that the normal mind of a mortal couldn't even fathom.

At first, Arthur was hesitant, but the allure of power and the promise of riches began to corrupt his heart. All of his ailments, the poverty, the hunger his family had to face, and the ridicule he received for being a peasant with nothing to claim as his own came to a boiling point as he surrendered himself to the power of Morgana. He soon came to the conclusion that he could now use his powers to commit crimes and slip

Unsolved Crimes

by undetected.

With the agreement made, requiring close to no convincing from Morgana's side, Arthur recited the dark incantation:

"In the depths of the night, by moon's silver light,

I call upon Morgana's power, fierce and bright.

With words of ancient lore, I now ignite,

A spell to summon magic beyond mortal sight."

"By Earth, by air, by fire, by sea, Morgana's power, come to me.

With mystic force and secrets untold,

Grant me the strength; make my desires unfold."

"From the realms of darkness,

from the depths of the night,

With your enchanted might, make all wrongs right.

Grant me your secrets, your knowledge untold,
Morgana's power, my destiny beholds."

With these words spoken, Morgana handed Arthur

Unsolved Crimes

the *Blackhold*, a book of incantations that has been revered in the Tobias family for centuries, with only the elderly most members being allowed to even know of it. The enchantment was finally cast, and Morgana's powers surged with an overwhelming blast of darkness. The forces of magic were now at Arthur's command, unleashed by the dark incantation.

He honed his mastery of the dark arts through the *Blackhold* for many months until, one day, Arthur employed his magical abilities under the cover of night to begin his spree of amassing wealth and influence. He used his powers of illusion to disguise his identity, making it impossible for anyone to connect him to the crimes that plagued Crestwood. He could slip into homes, pilfering valuables, and disappear into thin air, leaving no trace behind.

As time passed, Arthur's ill-gotten riches grew, and he began to use his influence to manipulate the village's affairs. He whispered in the ears of those in power, swaying their decisions to his advantage. With his knowledge of witchcraft, he became a formidable force, feared and respected by both the authorities and the villagers. But alas, no one knew of his true

Unsolved Crimes

powers and his bondage to Morgana.

Despite the growing unease in Crestwood, Arthur's true identity remained shrouded in mystery. Some believed him to be a guardian spirit, while others feared he was a malevolent force. The authorities, unable to prove his involvement in the crimes that plagued the village, were left powerless to stop him.

This led to the Tobias family being intrinsically linked to the dark arts for generations to come. Their family crest was a visage of Morgana, with a few words of the incantation stamped below the visage.

Throughout the years, knowledge of their link to Morgana eluded the multiple members of the Tobias family, with it being nothing but the family crest in the modern day. As was mentioned earlier, only the senior-most member of the Tobias family is made aware of Morgana as a sort of initiation, which, in the modern day, happens to be Minnie Tobias.

This has led to the dilution of Morgana's power in the Tobias family, with it only being controlled by the women members of the family. This mutation of their powers began around two hundred years ago with Eliza Tobias. Ever since her, only the female

Unsolved Crimes

descendants of the Tobias family have been able to call upon the powers of Morgana.

Lacey's Grandmother, Minnie, began practicing witchcraft at a young age with her mother and grandmother. The books and training, namely the Blackhold, were shared with when she came of age, long after she had become a skilled practitioner of the dark arts, for she was the eldest of her siblings and was destined to be the Tobias family elder one day.

The Tobias family had a unique talent that set them apart from others. Their go-to spell was the ability to warg, a technique that allowed them to take control of another entity in the astral realm. They were able to leave their physical bodies behind in the real world and enter the astral plane, where they could exert their influence over other people or even animals.

Though this act of warg was their preferred method, the Tobias family also could use astral projection. This was often employed in situations where they needed to gather information by spying on someone. With the ability to seamlessly move between the physical and astral realms, the Tobias family had a distinct advantage over their enemies.

Unsolved Crimes

The Tobias family, though deplorable, did look out for each other. Such was the case for William, Lacey's Uncle, when he killed his first wife, Layla, for cheating on him. Minnie and Beatrice knew that he was going to be caught with such a blatant murder, and since the males of the Tobias family could not call upon the powers of Morgana, they decided to do it for him.

They whisked away all the DNA evidence immediately, and on the day of the sale of the house he bought with Layla, Minnie cast a spell that created an illusion to make everyone think that his new wife, Diana, was actually Layla.

There have been multiple instances of the Tobias family using witchcraft to get away with crimes, such was the case with the murder, or supposed suicide, of Detective Lane, Sarah's father, who ended up dead the moment he was hot on the Tobias family's tail. *Curious.* Another example of the Tobias family's crimes is linked to the mysterious disappearance of Mr. Smith. Mr. Smith was a next-door neighbor of Minnie who made the grave mistake of poking his nose where it shouldn't have been. He heard the sound of chanting emanating from Minnie's house

Unsolved Crimes

one late night while he was going out for his nightly stroll around the neighborhood with his dog. He couldn't make the words out one-for-one, but he did hear something along the lines of *Morgana.*

The sound was coming from the basement, and Mr. Smith, in fatal curiosity, approached the outside door with his heart pounding out of his chest.

He and his dog were never seen again. It was a missing person's case that went cold. *Strange.*

With Minnie reaching the limit of her life in this mortal realm, the Tobias family is looking for a new inheritor after Beatrice.

What does Minnie have in store for Lacey?

Chapter 4

Born into Crime

The Talent of Deception

For many centuries, Lacey's ancestors made sure society kept them in high regard. A warm smile would appear on the faces of each and every member every time a stranger or even a neighbor passed by. It was a smile that always bewitched the watching eye—like a spell was cast on their minds, which created an illusion, leaving all of them in awe of Lacey's family.

This practice was passed down through the generations of Lacey's ancestors. They created their way in society by practicing these manipulative tactics. These tricks not only helped them live their life with great wealth and good health but also enabled them to master their witchcraft.

In other words, these techniques and practices allowed Lacey's ancestors and family to live according to their own terms and conditions with immense benefits and pleasures. A society where no

The Talent of Deception

single entity disliked or disregarded them, where they were admired and regarded as respected people, i.e., *A perfect society. FYI, such a society doesn't exist.*

This act of deceiving others through these bewitching tricks has helped Lacey's family in settling any conflict or issue that occurred in the neighborhood involving them. Whether it was William's horrendous act of murdering his first wife, Layla, in cold blood, which was hidden and swept away by Lacey's family with the help of the Tobias family, or it was eliminating Detective Lane, Sarah's father, Lacey's closest friend's father because he was very near to exposing the truth of Lacey's family. Then, whose death was conspired to appear as a suicide, i.e., *he died by hanging himself.* All of these conniving acts were done by the plotting and scheming of Minnie.

Minnie, a trained and well-crafted witch, was always involved in every act of deceit, manipulation, and cheating. Whatever the crime or atrocity dropped, she was always at the scene. From a different perspective, this can also be seen as an older member protecting her family from all the harsh realities of life, given that Minnie was the oldest of the family as well as Lacey's grandmother. But in this case, it is not only a

The Talent of Deception

matter of protecting one's own family but also about harming other people and their families for their own benefit and gains.

Sometimes, this trail of getting what you want and desire exceeded its limits when Minnie wounded her grandchild, Lacey, when she was only four years old. She executed her plan with Lacey's mother, Beatrice, to manipulate Lacey's father, Merlin. Minnie never felt any remorse after doing the devious act of cruelty.

This proves that the intoxication of power and perfection can turn a person into a vicious and powerful monster with the assurance of no consequences. While in this case, Minnie is also a witch who is in possession of many techniques, spells, and practices. The technique can make her and her whole family, except the children, exist in the astral realm, leaving their bodies in this real world to spy on the people who must be eliminated from their lives.

As shocking as it sounds, it is true. This practice has been followed by Lacey's ancestors since their beginning, i.e., hundreds of years. The witchcraft practices and techniques were taught to the children of Lacey's family from the age of fourteen.

The Talent of Deception

The children in Lacey's family have always kept their heads down in front of their elders. This is a prevailing practice among this family, passed down from their ancestors. It is like a tradition for the children to lower their heads when elders are speaking or teaching them something related to their ancestor's practices and crafts.

Since the earliest days of their youth, the children of Lacey's family have possessed an ardent yearning to embark upon their mystical journey of witchcraft. The very notion of reciting incantations, wielding magical powers, and attaining their heart's desires through the utterance of a few sacred words has consistently ignited a profound sense of excitement within them.

Yet, unbeknownst to these eager and wide-eyed youngsters, a shadowy undercurrent of darkness lurks within the annals of their ancestral lineage, exacting a toll upon the souls and minds of their forebears and kin. With its inherent brutality, this realm of darkness stealthily infiltrates the innocence and purity of these naive and tender spirits, tainting them with its corrupting influence.

The Talent of Deception

The children remain blissfully unaware of this foreboding aspect, for in their eyes, the Elders stand as the ultimate arbiters of truth and wisdom, holding sway over their understanding of the mystical arts.

However, Lacey was different. She still remembered how her grandmother pushed her down the stairs when she was only four years old. She was aware of her family's deceiving and conniving reality, which made them appear kind, gentle, and innocent family in the neighborhood. She was mindful of the kind of fake reality she was living in and how eagerly she wanted to get out of that manipulative and cunning environment.

According to the prevailing assumption within Lacey's family, it was widely believed that the children of her lineage were incapable of harnessing the powers of magic or engaging in the practice of casting spells until they reached the age of fourteen, a significant threshold marking their transition into adolescence.

However, unbeknownst to them, these young individuals possessed an inherent ability to unconsciously manifest a myriad of enchantments and sorceries. This latent gift, intricately intertwined

The Talent of Deception

with their genetic makeup, was passed down through successive generations, coursing through their very veins alongside the intricate strands of their DNA.

Thus, the family's unique connection to the mystical arts not only transcended mere learned knowledge but was instead an integral part of their inherited heritage, a legacy that remained dormant until the appointed age of awakening.

Lacey's maternal relatives believed that children from Lacey's family were born with the special ability to do magic. They could execute various magic practices and spells flawlessly, even without knowing it. They believed that fourteen was the age at which they were given training about witchcraft and its practices, consciously and attentively.

To this day, they hold this belief because of an incident they once saw from their own eyes. When Lacey was six years old, she was playing in the garden, which was full of flowers. The garden was near their home. She was playing with her dolls and talking with the flowers while touching and smelling them softly. Then, she stood up and went to the area where the flowers had withered and fallen down. Their color was faded, and they were falling out of

The Talent of Deception

their branches. Aunt Diana was watching from her bench while Lacey stood in the garden for ten minutes looking around. Then, she made some hand gestures, like swaying both hands in a circular motion. While she was doing this, she was constantly chanting some words which were long and difficult to figure out. But, after ten minutes, that withered area blossomed and colorful with beautiful flowers, blooming with their vibrant and vivid color. This made Lacey's aunt shocked and perplexed, and she inquired about it from Lacey. However, she had no idea what she did or said.

Lacey, who is now in the phase of becoming an adult, is fully aware of her family and their deceiving outlook on the world. She wants to free herself from these ill practices and traditions. But, her grandmother, Minnie, is slowly going toward her end and wants to pass on these practices and traditions to a young and innocent blood, i.e., Lacey.

Minnie was attentive toward Lacey's rebellious behavior, and she knew that Lacey would be hard to capture and convince. She was not like her other grandchildren in the family, as Lacey was someone who was exposed to these practices and techniques

The Talent of Deception

when she was only a child. She will not easily be swayed into accepting this realm.

However, Minnie is also an expert at getting what she wants in her own manipulative and deceiving ways. She knows how to occupy Lacey in this family's matters and never let her free from her roots. Minnie knows the perfect target to manipulate and convince Lacey. An option that Lacey will always take and will never refuse or ignore—*Sarah, her closest friend.*

Minnie, with her family and relatives, perhaps has an evil and manipulative plan that will force Lacey to take her family's traditions and practices seriously and become the next heir of it, by hook or *crook.*

Chapter 5

Born into Crime

Leaving Evil

Breaking away from her evil relatives and enjoying life without the presence of criminals was a prospect Lacey was looking quite forward to in her not-so-distant future.

This was because she always knew and acknowledged that she had to keep her chin up and go through life in stride. The unfortunate truth, though, was that she also knew staying happy simply wasn't possible with the presence of such evil in her life.

Henceforth, she had decided that once she was 18 years old, she would get her own place to stay, a place far away from her ties to the Tobias Family.

The day was nigh out of virtue of the fact that Lacey had just graduated high school. Strangely enough, Beatrice threw a graduation party for her at her house, inviting multiple members of the Tobias

Leaving Evil

family. Her cousins, aunts, and uncles were all there. Yet, the strangest addition of all was Merlin, Lacey's father, who brought his new wife Pamela along.

This addition was strange, namely due to the fact that Beatrice and Merlin didn't have the best of histories, so the fact that she decided to call him and bring his enlightened presence close to the Tobias Family's dark shadow was a strange decision, to say the least.

Lacey still had her suspicions, though, for she knew how her mother, Beatrice, functioned. She knew Beatrice was simply an extension of Lacey's grandmother, Minnie, who would *never* want Merlin anywhere near the family.

Lacey rationalized this instance by assuming that the party was a front. It wasn't really a graduation party; it was an initiation. Multiple Tobias family members were here to size Lacey up, as she was next in line after Beatrice to inherit the throne of the Tobias Family head.

Lacey knew the only reason Beatrice and Minnie even *considered* the prospect of calling Merlin was that Lacey would have never agreed to the party unless her father was there. But alas, that was the truth of life for

Leaving Evil

Lacey. She had grown used to all the lies and deception that were the norm for her maternal side of her family.

The party itself, strangely, seemed to be a normal, if not fun, affair. There were several elders of the family sat around on a table playing cards. This usually served as a front for their family conferences, no doubt to explore their next evil schemes. In moments like these, Lacey felt like she had an actual family and not a group of criminals that surrounded her.

The festivities continued through the whole day, with many of the members of the Tobias family exchanging stares with Lacey, no doubt to see if she was worthy of the Tobias Family mantle. Games were played, beers were drunk, and gossip was exchanged.

Toward the end of a tiring day, all the guests had seemingly left, including Merlin and Pamela. Minnie, being ever the heavy drinker, found herself still at the table where the Tobias family elders were meeting.

In her drunken splendor, she called her granddaughter over to spend some *quality time*, "Come here and crack open a cold one with me." She beckoned Lacey. Apparently, Minnie had forgotten

Leaving Evil

that this wasn't Lacey's birthday and that she wasn't 18 yet. Lacey was going to turn 18 a few months after that point, but she was still underage at that moment.

Lacey, unfortunately, forgot how Minnie exploited people and accepted the individual under the assumption that Minnie didn't really have anything sinister in mind.

Minnie actually used this opportunity to probe Lacey's thoughts on the extended family members of the Tobias Family. Exploiting the fact that Lacey still didn't have a grasp of her limits towards alcohol, Minnie took notes as Lacey opened up more and more. But after a while, Minnie seemed to be warming up to Lacey because the two were actually getting to know each other. They had never had a human conversation before, but this time, it felt like they could each forget their responsibilities and be humans. They could be what they actually were: grandmother and granddaughter. Minnie felt a sense of pride in herself for Lacey, not only because she had just graduated, but she also felt proud of the way Lacey carried herself in front of the other members of the Tobias family. She felt a sense of completion that she was passing the mantle down to her granddaughter, who seemed

Leaving Evil

more than just a qualified candidate. Minnie knew that the family would be in good hands if Lacey took the mantle and title in stride.

She knew Lacey had a stronger connection to witchcraft due to her being the daughter of Merlin and Beatrice, and she could harness the darkness *and* the light.

Minnie knew Lacey was special.

Five Weeks Later

Lacey was finally 18 years old, and after years of saving, doing odd jobs, and whatnot, she finally had enough to rent her own place.

After moving into her quaint little apartment, Lacey was finally free of her relatives. Her apartment wasn't all too shabby for a young lady such as Lacey, but it made do. After all, she wasn't looking to sit on the lap of luxury; she just wanted to get away from it all. Coming from a life of crime, the restlessness had settled into Lacey's mind.

Living with a family of murderers, thieves, and evil-doers, Lacey yearned to leave the family home. She knew the risks of staying with the family and that if

Leaving Evil

she had remained there; her mortal existence would've been threatened by her own kin.

The first day, when Lacey moved into her new apartment, she felt free from family conspiracies for the first time in her life. No more would Lacey be associated with the fiends and thralls conjured by Beatrice or Minnie's curses bestowed onto the family's enemies. Her life was her own, and she could now decide how to pave the way for her future.

Lacey decided to decorate her small apartment to resonate with her kind-hearted personality, which she inherited from Merlin. She never was an evil-doer from the moment she realized her powers. The same cannot be said for the rest of the Tobias family, though. They demanded more from her because Lacey was unique. Lacey's apartment balcony opened to the beautiful view of the modern city of Pinewood – a city full of opportunities.

As the saying goes,

> *"No soul sleeps hungry in the city of Pinewood."*

The place was a bustling and contemporary environment that allowed individuals to explore their potential. The cozy apartment comprised three rooms

Leaving Evil

in total, with one room left vacant by Lacey as she had not yet decided on its purpose. The other two rooms consisted of a standard bedroom with an attached bathroom and a kitchen area with a small passage leading to the corridor and the exit.

One day, Lacey decided to go for a stroll in the city. She grabbed her satchel, donned her jacket, and proceeded to the apartment's exit. She had only closed her apartment door when she heard some utterly strange noises. The noises were coming from the apartment next door, which she thought was unoccupied.

Ignoring the noise, Lacey hurried toward the stairs. The noises spelled trouble, which Lacey didn't wish to concern herself with. Not yet, at least. She descended from the staircase and continued to do so till her apartment was a distant sight. The city of Pinewood was about ten minutes away from Lacey's apartment, so she decided to take a walk.

Thinking about the strange noises along the way, Lacey's concentration had dwindled, and she kept walking. Lacey bumped into a gentleman called Gale, who appeared to be a bearded man with a tattoo on his forehead, wearing an overcoat and a fedora. The

Leaving Evil

impact snapped Lacey back into the present situation.

When she bumped into Gale, he had dropped the eggs he was carrying. Shocked, Lacey leaped forward with a helping hand, but it was already too late. To Lacey's good fortune, Gale was a forgiving man.

Lacey hurriedly checked her satchel and gave Gale some money she had saved. Gale denied this offer with a smile and commended Lacey for her generosity.

"Don't sweat it; it happens to the best of us," Gale said as he slowly turned his back toward Lacey and walked away. The world hadn't been too kind for Lacey before this. All she had known was lies and deception. Coming to grips with the situation, Lacey, too, started to walk toward the city.

Pinewood was a bright city where everyone was someone. Lacey stood in awe. There was music, people, and lights, and the town of Pinewood was brimming with life. Never did Lacey witness such wonders. It was then she realized that moving away from her relatives was the wisest decision she had made.

Slowly approaching a café, Lacey glared at the city's

Leaving Evil

skylines. Everyone in Pinewood she saw seemed too busy. Enthralled by her environs, Lacey took a deep breath of relief. The café's here.

Lacey took the table closest to the window so she could continue gazing at the vistas. The waitress approached her, and Lacey ordered a cup of tea. A man of mystery sat at the distant corner of the café, where the lights were dim.

Oblivious of his presence, Lacey took her tea, tucked the money under the saucer, and walked out of the café. It was almost evening, so she decided to return to her apartment. Safely walking back to her apartment, ascending the stairs, and reaching her floor, she could still hear the sounds coming from the door next to hers.

Only this time, they were a tad louder. There was agony in these noises. It was as if someone was tied down and was trying to break free. Something was completely off. Lacey contained her whims and went inside her apartment. She threw away her jacket and satchel and rushed toward her bed, tired yet content with the sights she had seen.

The following day, there was a knock-on Lacey's

Leaving Evil

door. It was the police. Lacey was anxious as she thought they were here due to her ties with the Tobias family. But to her surprise, the officers were investigating another case entirely. The sounds next door had stopped, and what came next could very well be a shocking reveal for Lacey. The officers informed her that they found evidence of an evil ritualistic practice in the apartment next door, the details of which were highly graphic. After questioning Lacey, the officers advised her to remain vigilant and to report to the authorities for anything unusual.

In utter shock, Lacey instantly realized that this was no mere coincidence. It was a warning. The Tobias family elders did not forget her; simply distancing herself doesn't guarantee her safety. There was a bigger scheme in motion. *But what?*

Lacey decided to enroll in a career academy to obtain certification upon completing a 500-hour program covering extensive computer platform training and administration functions. Additionally, the academy offered job placement assistance to students upon graduation, and Lacey was able to take advantage of a Pell Grant to help cover the costs of the program.

Life went on without too many trials and tribulations,

Leaving Evil

with Lacey almost enjoying her life as it was, but all was not as it seemed, for strange happenings were persistent in her life. She just chose to ignore them, for her sake, and the people that surrounded her, for she was still in touch with Sarah Lane, and she was terrified of what the Tobias family would do to her if she remained her fiery self back in Crestwood.

Six Years Later

It was an important day—the day Lacey would take off from work to attend Tobias' family reunion dinner. Beatrice had called Lacey a little earlier so the immediate family could enjoy a 'nice lunch' before the festivities.

Lacey got to her childhood home around 12 P.M., a little ahead of schedule, but at least she didn't have to meet anyone because everyone was still out for work. The last thing she wanted was any unnecessary interactions with her family of criminals.

She had peace for a few hours, or so she thought because Franklin got home early as well and was surprised to see Lacey there. He was also surprised to know that she still had the keys to the house.

Leaving Evil

"Fancy seeing you here, your Holiness," Franklin said with an abundance of sarcasm, alluding to the fact that the Tobias family wasn't delighted with Lacey's decision to cut her ties with them.

"Thanks for the hospitality. I'm surprised you haven't kicked me out yet," Lacey said with an equal amount of sarcasm.

"Nonsense! We cherish your presence whenever we can; after all, we have so little time with you left! I doubt you'll even make it to 25!" A chill went down Lacey's spine with this statement. Coming from someone so deeply interlinked with the Tobias family, these words were not to be taken lightly.

"Welcome home, Lacey," Franklin said with a sinister tone as he went to his room, leaving Lacey dumbfounded.

Was he serious about what he just said, or was it just an intimidation tactic?

Chapter 6

Born into Crime

Suffering After Leaving Criminals

After four years of living away from the influences of the Tobias Family home, Lacey was content with how she was living her life. The real factor wasn't the fact that she was living an inherently cushy life. Rather, it was the reality that she was living her life her way. What was being done by her elders had no bearing on her, or so she thought. It was a warm summer evening when Lacy and her friends decided to head out for a night of fun.

They piled into the car, the music blaring and the laughter filling the air. Lacey sat in the passenger seat; her excitement palpable. They had no idea that their lives were about to change in an instant.

As they drove down the familiar winding road, a sudden flash of headlights blinded Lacey's friend, the driver. In a split second, everything spiraled out of

Suffering After Leaving Criminals

control. The screeching of tires, the sound of metal colliding, and the shattering of glass filled the air.

When Lacey regained consciousness, she found herself in a hospital bed, surrounded by concerned faces. The doctors explained the severity of her injuries: a broken neck and a cracked skull. The news hit her like a ton of bricks. Her dreams, her plans, and her vibrant spirit suddenly seemed distant and unattainable. She once again felt the despair that she was accustomed to when she used to live with the Tobias Family. This despair almost captivated her to the point where she was about to panic, but a level of warmth resonated from one corner of the room that wasn't in her view.

Merlin was standing there, looking more than just slightly concerned for her, "You've been out for a whole day, honey. What on Earth happened?"

"I... I don't remember." Lacey replied, holding back the tears. "Dad, I don't know what to do. The doctors told me I have permanent damage.".

"Yes, I've been made aware. But you have to listen to me, Lacey. This isn't the end of the world. You have to believe me. This could have ended much worse."

Suffering After Leaving Criminals

Merlin said, trying to show her a light at the end of the tunnel.

"Damn it. This is definitely something Minnie and Mom did. Dad, I just know they were behind this. Maybe that's why Franklin said I won't even make it to 25. They planned all of this. They've been trying to kill me since I've been a kid! What the hell do they want from me? Why won't they just leave me alone?" Lacey was at the end of her rope at this point.

"Lace, you know there's no way to prove that. We can't do anything about it. You already know I would be the first one to jump at them, but there's nothing we can do," Merlin replied.

"I know, Dad, but I'm just so tired of it. I don't *want* anything to do with them. Why can't they just leave me alone?" Lacey implored Merlin.

"Have you ever thought about how they never meddle in my matters? Don't you ever wonder how I haven't earned myself an early grave with how much they hate me?" Merlin was alluding to the solution Lacey was looking for.

"See, the thing is, they draw their powers from the darkness. The depths of evil are rooted strongly in

Suffering After Leaving Criminals

their hearts, and the only way to counter that is to be one with your higher power: *the light*. Lacey, you need to embrace God and let him guide you. I say this because he's the only force in this entire world that can counter the darkness. You need to solidify this link with him so that he can heal you, and not just that, but also so that he can make you stronger."

"So, what you're saying is that just because you believe in god, Minnie and Mom can't do anything to you?" Lacey asked.

"Yup, that's pretty much the gist of it, so how about once you're discharged, I teach you the ropes?" Merlin replied back.

"That… that would be nice," Lacey said, with a higher degree of hope in life than ever before.

Days turned into weeks, and weeks turned into months as Lacey fought a grueling battle for her recovery. The road to healing was filled with pain, frustration, and countless hours of rehabilitation. But Lacey was determined, refusing to let the accident and her tie to her family define her.

A few months later

Suffering After Leaving Criminals

Lacey stood at the hospital entrance, her heart pounding with a mix of excitement and trepidation. After months of grueling rehabilitation, she was finally discharged. The journey ahead was uncertain, but she was determined to step into the world once again, armed with newfound strength and resilience.

As Lacey walked out of the hospital doors, she noticed her father, Merlin, waiting for her. Merlin was a man of gentle wisdom, a beacon of support throughout her recovery. His eyes welled up with tears as he embraced his daughter, feeling the weight of her triumph against all odds.

"Welcome back, Lace," Merlin whispered, his voice filled with a mix of pride and relief. "You've shown incredible strength, and I know your journey is far from over."

Lacey smiled, grateful for her father's support. She knew that her healing was not just a result of medical intervention but also a result of the power of love and faith. Little did she realize that Merlin had something profound to share with her, something that would shape her perception of her own journey:

The power of faith.

Suffering After Leaving Criminals

In the days that followed, Lacey embraced her father's teachings, finding solace and strength in her faith. She embarked on a spiritual journey, exploring the incredible power of prayer and experiencing the firm love of a higher power. With every passing day, Lacey's belief in miracles grew stronger, like a flickering flame becoming a blazing fire.

As Lacey stepped back into the world, she carried with her a newfound purpose, a sense of resolve that went beyond her physical limitations. She became a shining beacon of light, pushing back against the darkness that threatened to swallow her through her family. Guided by God and inspired by her father's wisdom, she knew deep within that she possessed the fortitude to confront any obstacle that lay in her path.

With unyielding determination, Lacey ventured forth, her heart brimming with faith, love, and a fierce determination to shape her own destiny. She refused to allow her past to define her, steadfastly rejecting the shadows of her family's legacy. Each step she took was a testament to her solid belief in the healing power of God as she strode forward into a future teeming with boundless opportunities and infinite possibilities.

Chapter 7

Born into Crime

Surviving a Life with Criminals

Guided by her newfound connection to her higher power, Lacey lived a life of happiness, with a reformed outlook and life without the influence of the Tobias Family hanging over her head. She went to church, read the bible daily, and ensured that her connection with the Lord would stare her away from a dark path.

But all was not as simple as it seemed, for Minnie still had sinister plans for her. Minnie knew that she was not long for this world. Despite her magical prowess, she knew she had to leave the Tobias family lineage clean, for her family was the direct descendent of Arthur Tobias, not an offshoot branch from the family tree like many of their relatives.

This meant that Minnie left no stone unturned in her quest to bring Lacey back to the family by any means

Surviving a Life with Criminals

necessary. She knew Lacey was potent in her magic, and she knew Lacey had the highest ceiling when it came to the dark arts, even though the blood of Merlin tainted her.

Minnie was determined to bring her granddaughter back, leveraging the fact that she had suffered a severe head injury. She decided to take matters into her own hands by casting spells to convince Lacey that she could not lead her own life and needed a psychological examination. Minnie wanted to provide a basis for documenting Lacey's ability to care for herself and make responsible decisions.

During the testing, Minnie cast a spell on everyone involved, including Lacey, encouraging her to come home safe from the doctors if she was unsatisfied with the results. Minnie felt that Lacey needed to overestimate the extent of the permanent physical damage she had suffered and survived.

However, Lacey was not on board with the idea and pushed back against it. She did not want to prove that her mind was working well and refused to continue the examination. Despite this setback, Minnie refused to give up and continued to cast spells on several neighbors and friends to fulfill her plan. She was

Surviving a Life with Criminals

determined to bring Lacey back to the family and make her inherit the throne as the Tobias Family head.

One other instance was Minnie gaining control of Gale, Lacey's neighbor. It was just another day. Gale was walking back to his apartment with his usual groceries. During one of her visits to Lacey's house, Minnie did see Gale and considered him the perfect candidate to warg into because he was a large, burly man who could easily overpower Lacey.

The moment Gale was entering his apartment, Gale suddenly blacked out. His eyes rolled to the back of his head as he collapsed, but he caught his fall. The only thing was he wasn't the one who saw his fall. It was actually Minnie in the body of Gale.

Minnie's spell was a success, as a sinister smile came across her face, or rather, Gale's face, as she started controlling his body and took confident strides towards her apartment, g-136, feeling her plans soon coming to fruition. A sudden force jolted her awake as she reached for the door handle.

She was back in her own body, in a cold sweat. Something had forcefully pushed her out of the astral

Surviving a Life with Criminals

realm. Her heavy breathing accentuated her confusion. A cup of coffee was all she was having at Lacey's apartment when she heard a loud thud outside her door. She felt something was wrong. As she approached the door, she looked at the Cross hanging from it and suddenly felt a warm feeling of comfort.

She cautiously opened the door and was surprised to see Gale lying on the floor but slowly regaining consciousness.

"Uh, Gale? What are you doing here?" Lacey asked, utterly perplexed.

"I... I don't know... One second, I was walking into my apartment with my groceries. The next, I'm here on the floor in front of *your* apartment!" He said, just as confused.

"Looks like someone had one hell of a night, huh?" Lacey faked her confusion as she started putting the pieces together.

"Yeah, I guess so. I'm really sorry about that, and I meant no harm. I have no idea what came over me." Gale said with shame all over his face.

"Oh, it's alright, Gale. Just... lay off the excessive

Surviving a Life with Criminals

benders." Lacey jokingly said that Gale wouldn't feel responsible.

"Will do, ma'am, will do." He let out a nervous laugh and fled the scene.

As Lacey went back inside, she turned around to look at the Cross hanging off her door and said, "Thank you."

***

A determined woman, Minnie refused to give up on her quest to bring her granddaughter, Lacey, back to the Tobias family. After a series of unsuccessful attempts, Minnie discovered an ancient artifact hidden in the family storage room. It was called the Staff of Ashbala, said to be wielded by the dark Lord Morgana, and it was believed to have the power to manipulate the minds of those who possessed it. Minnie saw this as her last hope to control Lacey's decisions and actions.

Minnie's heart raced as she held the staff in her hand, feeling its powerful energy coursing through her veins. She approached Lacey with the staff, hoping to use its powers to sway her granddaughter's thoughts and bring her back to the family. However, as she

Surviving a Life with Criminals

attempted to use the artifact, her hopes were dashed - Lacey remained utterly unaffected by the staff's power.

She was shell-shocked - she had never encountered anyone with such strong willpower. She tried repeatedly, using all the knowledge she had acquired about the staff's power, but to no avail. Lacey was protected by a divine shield that prevented any form of magical manipulation.

Minnie's frustration grew as she realized her failure. She had been so sure that this artifact was the answer to her troubles, but she now knew that her granddaughter's strength was too great to be overcome by any form of magic.

***

Lacey's strong connection with her higher power is a source of frustration for Minnie, who is determined to break it. She resorts to the use of dark magic despite knowing very well the risks involved. Minnie delves deep into the forbidden arts, seeking a way to sever Lacey's divine protection and gain control over her. With bated breath, she performs a powerful ritual that involves invoking dark forces and channeling

Surviving a Life with Criminals

their energy toward Lacey.

As Minnie completes the ritual, the atmosphere becomes charged with an ominous energy, and a sudden gust of wind blows through the room. Lacey stands motionless, her eyes closed, as if in deep prayer. Suddenly, a blinding light engulfs her, revealing a radiant presence that repels the dark energies. The light is so bright that Minnie has to shield her eyes. She can feel the power of the divine presence, and it fills her with a sense of awe and fear.

Minnie realizes too late that she has made a grave mistake. The ritual backfires, and the dark energies that she sought to control turn against her. She feels herself weakening as the energies drain her of her strength. She tries to fight back, but it's no use. The radiant presence surrounding Lacey is too powerful and repels the dark forces completely. She is left defeated once again, her plans in ruins.

***

Motivated by a strong desire to sever Lacey's connection with her higher power once and for all, Minnie sets out on a dangerous mission. She firmly believes that if she can manage to separate Lacey's

Surviving a Life with Criminals

soul from her body, she will be able to manipulate and control her without any divine intervention. In order to accomplish this, Minnie gathers a group of dark sorcerers from the notorious Tobias family. Together, they perform a complex and intricate ritual to successfully extract Lacey's soul.

But just as the ritual reaches its climactic moment, the room is suddenly filled with a blinding light, leaving Minnie and her accomplices startled and amazed. Standing before them is an ethereal figure radiating immense power—an angelic being sent by her higher power to protect Lacey. The angel's divine presence overwhelms the dark magic, shattering Minnie's plans. With a simple wave of its hand, the angel dispels the dark sorcerers and breaks the connection between them and Lacey's soul.

Minnie watches in horror as Lacey's soul returns to her body, more resilient than ever. The failed attempt leaves Minnie humiliated and defeated, realizing that Lacey's bond with her higher power remains unbreakable no matter what dark powers she wields.

***

Minnie uses the power of illusion as a potent tool in

Surviving a Life with Criminals

her mission to return Lacey to the Tobias family. In order to fulfill her objective, She constructs a sophisticated and subtle fantasy world that is intended to satiate Lacey's cravings and convince her that going back to the Tobias family is her actual destiny. Then Lacey finds herself losing herself in Minnie's imaginative world, losing the ability to distinguish between fact and fantasy.

Nevertheless, Lacey's faith in her higher power allows her to look past the delusion and grasp reality. Lacey escapes Minnie's hold and seizes control of her life with the aid of her religion. When Lacey becomes clearer, the deception breaks, and Minnie loses once more.

***

In a desperate move, Minnie turns to a powerful and ancient curse called the "Curse of Binding." The dark spell is known to forcibly bind individuals to their lineage, making it impossible for them to break away from their family's corrupting influence. Minnie casts the curse on her, driven by her desire to sever Lacey's connection with her higher power and ensure her return to the family.

Surviving a Life with Criminals

As the curse tightens its grip on Lacey, a sudden and unexpected divine intervention takes place, causing the curse's magic to unravel. The intervention frees Lacey from the curse's hold, thereby thwarting Minnie's plan to control her.

The failure of the curse to bind Lacey leaves Minnie defeated, but she refuses to give up on her quest to establish her dark power and authority over Lacey. Her ultimate goal is to groom Lacey to take over the family head title, even if it means resorting to the most sinister tactics.

***

Minnie was at her wit's end. Her time was soon nigh, and she only wanted to make sure the Tobias family would prosper. Unfortunately for her, all of her plans were thwarted throughout the months and years. She failed with her attempts in the astral realm.

She was still determined, leading to her throwing caution to the wind and going to Lacey's apartment herself.

She was drained from all the magic she had employed to sink her fangs into Lacey, so eventually, she resorted to her last avenue: The Blood of Morgana. In

Surviving a Life with Criminals

a chalice, hidden deep within the Tobias family compound, laid a secret elixir, whose knowledge was only given to the head of the family, who, in this case, was Minnie.

The elixir was potent. It had a sinister effect. Once consumed, the person who drank it would become a vessel for Morgana for two hours, but it came at a hefty price: death. The vessel of Morgana would have to trade off the remaining years of their life to harness Morgana's unbound power, something Minnie was more than ready to do. In return, Morgana, hosting the body for those two hours, would fulfill only one wish for the host, as a sort of *dying wish*, and Minnie's dying wish was to capture Lacey.

More than happy with the conditions, as long as it meant success, Minnie chugged the elixir. This was her last attempt, whether she succeeded or failed.

In Minnie's body, Morgana immediately materialized in the hallway outside Lacey's apartment and walked toward it.

Lacey's firm faith in her higher power radiated with a strength that Morgana could not comprehend. As Minnie, in tandem with Morgana's control, stood in

Surviving a Life with Criminals

Lacey's apartment, fueled by the potent elixir and consumed by her desire for power, she prepared herself to reveal the depths of her malice.

But as she unleashed her most wicked intentions, Lacey remained steadfast, her eyes filled with an inner light. With a calm but resolute voice, Lacey spoke words that echoed through the room, piercing Minnie's very core.

"You should leave now and stay away," Lacey said, her voice carrying an authority that surpassed Minnie's dark powers. "Your power is no good here. This is more than my home; my higher power lives in me and will forever have authority over your evil ways." Minnie recoiled, stunned by the power and conviction in Lacey's words. The darkness that had consumed her began to crumble under the weight of Lacey's faith as Morgana left her body, defeated by the power of Lacey's faith in her higher power. The apartment seemed to shift, the atmosphere transforming into an aura of divine protection.

At that moment, Minnie realized the futility of her efforts. No amount of dark magic or desperate measures could prevail against the untiring connection Lacey had with her higher power. The veil

Surviving a Life with Criminals

of illusion that Minnie had crafted around herself shattered, revealing the truth she had been unwilling to face.

Defeated and drained, Minnie's body trembled as the remaining moments of the elixir's effect ticked away. She understood now that her pursuit of power and control had only led her down a path of destruction and despair.

With a heavy heart and a newfound clarity, Minnie retreated from Lacey's apartment and resigned herself to her fate as she would die in just an hour. The battle between Minnie's darkness and Lacey's faith had reached its conclusion, and confidence had emerged triumphant.

As the door closed behind Minnie, she looked at Lacey one last time and recalled her graduation party, "No matter what happens, I'm still proud of you, Lacey." She uttered this and disappeared, using the last morsel of power left in her.

Lacey felt calm inside but was still left with the understanding that her journey towards freedom from her evil elders was far from over. She had finally ended the fight with her grandmother, and that

Surviving a Life with Criminals

meant a different member of the Tobias Family would take over in Minnie's place.

Lacey survived evil time and time again throughout the next thirty or so years. She continues to live well with her faith in her higher power.

Lacey continued to survive the Evil of the Tobias Family throughout her entire life by holding on tight to her relationship with God and her unbreakable Faith.